My Body Didn't Come Before Me

My Body Didn't Come Before Me

POEMS

Kuhu Joshi

SPEAKING
TIGER

SPEAKING TIGER BOOKS LLP
125A Ground Floor, Shahpur Jat,
New Delhi 110049

First published by Speaking Tiger Books in paperback in 2023

Copyright © Kuhu Joshi 2023

ISBN: 978-93-5447-585-6
eISBN: 978-93-5447-583-2

10 9 8 7 6 5 4 3 2 1

CONTENTS

MY BODY
DIDN'T COME
BEFORE ME

I tell myself I am beautiful

                    I am twisted
        and turned. Moving
                in to and out of. My bones

know no direction.
        They choose not to limit
            to straightness. Rivers

                        that curve and meander
        to anywhere. They twist
            inside me

trying to find their way.
        They push
            and change every day.

                    They grow
        into a deeper S. And I tell myself
            I am beautiful

so I do not feel the need
        to be normal. I tell myself
            I am beautiful

                    so I do not feel the need
        to be something I am not.

The day of the fitting

I enter the basement

of the Spinal Injuries Hospital. It is white,

walls and a bed and a curtain. Mom is holding my hand.

There is a doctor, also in white. He does not look at me.
He says namaste to Mom.

He dips his hand into a tub of white liquid, pouring more
white powder into it.

She will have to take her clothes off, he says while mixing.

I am in blue bloomers and white baniyaan. *Keep this on,*
Mom says inside my ears.

The doctor pulls open the curtain and points to a stool. I
sit on it and he shuts out Mom.

Suddenly, wet on my side-ribs, wet under my breasts, wet

under my armpits, wet on my abdomen. His hands are cold,

as they rub wet all over. He says, *keep your arms out to
the side and stay still.*

White liquid turns solid around my torso. I do not breathe
from fear of cracking.

Mom is peeking through a gap in the curtain.

Next step, I am lying face-down on the white bed. The hands are messing

wet on my back ribs. I smell cement and Mom's perfume.

I smell the doctor's sweat as he moves.

I am a mummy, front and back. He takes a saw and I am alive.

He cuts open the plaster. I stand so he can take it off me.

In his hands, the skeleton of my body. In his hands

the silence of my spine, white and hollow. Mom is still standing.

And so am I.

Arms out, naked.

In this one you win

(For Mom)

In this one you are
cutting squares out of blue fabric
that you matched with my school dress.
You are sewing up the edges.
The doctor said twenty-two hours:
one for bathing and one of my choosing.
He gave us two hours outside the cage.

In this one I tell you
I won't go to school anymore.
'You can't make me.' I shut the door.
I think a lot about the cold, wet plaster.
And the hands of the doctor
moulding it around my waist.

In this one you are driving home the cage
sitting next to me in the car
and my tears in your rear-view mirror.

In this one you are showing me
how to wrap the blue fabric on the iron ring.
Soft cotton asking me to live.
'It looks just like a scarf!'
I think maybe it's true. No one will know
I have rods up my chest and back.

In this one you are sitting in the MRI room
while I lie inside the machine.
The car key flies from your hand
and smacks the round giant.

In Nani's house

I push my weight
against the sturdy swing-door
of Nani's house.
My eyes catch white and grey:

Nana's pebble garden
where we would discover
fat pieces of rock. *Khadiya.*

We would write our names
and make animal faces
on small slates.
My baby brother and I.

Papa isn't here.
Mom is cutting fruit.
Inside, on her favourite chair,
Nani is chopping kaddu.
She hobbles back and forth from the kitchen.
Nana's radio plays sitar.

My brother and I are free.
We take *khadiya* and draw our future.
We wipe the details we do not like.

It is dark when we hop back inside,
pick our places at the dinner table.
I, an astronaut,
digging into mango chutney.
He, a mountain,
birthing pahadi raita.

Papa isn't here

and we are free to dream
in Nani's house.

Yoga in a saree

Kamala likes it. Thighs stretching, petticoat breathing,
feet pressing together in a namaskara
to brown dogs licking their paws, scratching mud
for today's breakfast.

Adhomukhasvanasana:
Kamala mimics their pose, elongating into
the downward-facing dog. Kamala feels the wind tickling the skin
on her lower back,
sweeping her braid off her hip to greet
her right breast. Kamala enjoys

opening her chest. Challenging five little hooks to battle
gravity as it cradles her breasts.
Kamala likes this crackling of bones, spreading of legs,
tightening of palms, lengthening of neck,

this inhalation-exhalation, this dipping of butt, this bending of
spine, this clenching
of gut, this flaring of collar bone,
only for herself.
Kamala carries nine yards around her body,

spins them into Natarajasana, inverts them into Shirsasana.
Neatly tucked pleats
flying to the sky, palloo a green waving-flag brushing nose, then
thigh. Elbows
digging into the earth.
Sita incarnate, inverted.

Follow-up appointment

I had to spell it—h o p e l e ss n e ss
had to hiss my tongue twice, had to pronounce

right, had to say other words—tired empty hollow
like a bottomless bowl of brass, embossed,

till I tasted the bitter melt of Escitalopram
on the lilt of my tongue standing in front

of the pantry at work; till smiling good morning
colleagues watched my eyebrows knit but didn't

ask what is this medicine? I had to hear it
from the lady doctor, wise in her metallic zipper

coat, saying let us not taper anymore.
Had to hear my name—Kuhu—had to whisper

Kuhu down my throat, had to rub my palm in circles
around my navel, had to feel the bed flatten

underneath my spine, had to hear her say—Kuhu
you take care of yourself.

A girl. Scoliotic.

I don't remember her name.

I remember her Instagram handle. sco.lio
_something. I remember clicking on her

to compare her

curves to mine. On the grid, she appeared in black and white
X-rays. Her spinal cord a perfect S shape

in one, lodged with bullets

in another. *Wait. Those are not bullets.*
I squeezed my screen

into iron nails, iron bars,
iron nails screwing together iron bars,

something a doctor might draw, a bad
little scrawl, her spinal cord lodged

left and right with bullets.
I keep saying bullets. They were nails

and they were finger-sized, and they were inside
her, sitting next to her kidney, brushing the walls

of her intestine. They looked tight. Like corsets
on drugs. Dug into the pink

fleshiness across her ribcage,

deeper and deeper at the fat

portion of her S. When I saw her, my first thought

was relief.
Second, was tightness.

Third was my palm unhooking
my vertebrae. Fourth, the absence of bullets.

Fifth, my curve
was never that curvy.

Sixth, my god, she is so skinny.
Seventh, how will she have sex?

Eighth, when she moves,
do the bullets move with her?

All. those years. of breathing

into the belts around my chest. How tight
they had to be. There could be no gaps

for breath
to float in or float out. The truth is

it hurt. The truth

is my arm twisted when I pulled on the buckle to make it tight.
more tight. more
tight. The truth is I could not

stop. They were never tight

enough. The truth is my bras got loosened, old,
that I never got to buy sexy ones.
Not violet sequin, not auburn lace. The mannequin women
jut out their breasts. The truth is my rib cage
had lines. That I learnt to name
some shades of pink. Salmon? Flamingo? Hot-pink?

The truth is not breathing
becomes easier. That my boobs popped

between the belts, that I was only twelve. The truth is
I never felt sexy. The truth is Vikas ji

stared at my boobs. So did the other men.
The truth is I deserved it. Deserved to be strapped

back into shape. Now, my ribs
feel everything.

Pooja

Panditji can sit on our divan but Lekha cannot.
She cooks food for us and he offers it to the Gods.

I don't tell Dadi I am on my period. Steal
pooa off the prasad ki thali. Dadi is making me carry

banana leaves to the pooja room. They are larger
than her torso and will be used for the havan.

Lekha is not allowed to touch them. Bua
comes at 2 p.m. sharp to prepare halwa-prasad. Lekha sits

in the balcony next to the washing machine,
playing with her little niece. Aaru is three

and has a boy-cut now. I call her inside, offer my stool.
This time when she leaves, she says bye-bye to me.

Dadi is telling Lekha that Aaru will be a good sweeper.
'Even better than me?' Lekha is laughing. I want to say no.

Aaru will be whatever she wants. Like me,
she will go to office, wear running shoes.

Panditji is starting the pooja. A cone of incense
and some shloka. I sit knees-open on the stool,

elbows shooting out of my thighs,
hit rose petals at the Gods.

The protector of life

is a man. Larger
than building spires. Larger
than children wheeling bicycles,
children sprawling open with books
on the mud floor, larger than all
the scarves wrapped
around our breasts. The protector of life
is a man, and I
am not surprised. Neither are you.
I assure you. God
was a man too. This is what we
were given, you and I, Eves weeded out
of the garden of life. There was never a place
for the tang of apple, the hard
peel hitting against teeth
and the splashing of syrup
on breast. Eve had no bras
to strap her back. Now
they make them in garden colors,
lace and kitchen-ware and prints of magnolia.
Flowers blossom on breasts hidden
under layers. Protection was never made
for lifting our necks. And when we did,
curling our backs like stems
about to snap, there he was,
the protector, ready with metal
burning on his fingers.
When we pray on our knees
we do not pray to his mother.

The most beautiful part of every picture is the frame

When I think of limitations
I think of my father.

The table he got for me. Wood,
all shiny and new,
wood, all made by hand—
not his, but the *badhai*

who made the best tables in the world.

My father never went to buy groceries,
but he went to watch the *badhai*
making my table.

He sat on a stool and leaned
into writing pose, then
into reading pose.

He opened a newspaper
to see if the gap
was perfect enough,
to see if it was just right
for his girl, for her small

body to lean across
and reach
into the sea of vastness—mathematics, always
mathematics.

Then he went to the stationer
and found a notebook
with ruled paper. More limits
for sums that must go
line by line, *'is it not?*
Yes,
they go
like that

and when you carry over
a 9,
it floats
mid-way
between
two lines.'

Snails

My first blood was brown like poop
gone wrong. I didn't understand my bum
and why the poop kept falling out.

I took to eating more rice. Still the goopey
brown. Flecks some days, then a snail.
Enormous. I'd come home and bend over the sink,

scrubbing with a brush. The white bristles
turning to mud. For four days I took extra bloomers
in my school bag, didn't breathe much

on the bus back, gripped the seat
when we crossed over speed bumps.
On the fifth day, I showed two snails to Mum.

She stuck in a little white pad,
gave me a stack of old newspaper, and said,
don't drop them in the toilet. Then she opened

the *Illustrated Human Body*
and with her right index finger, she traced
what I didn't think could exist inside me.

Clockwork

I'm talking about people who popple and fall
and sneak up sneakily up your throat,
then bicker and backer while hacking at your jaws,
then sift and shift
down your throat pipe into your diaphragm, down & down
into your belly, its mouth, before beginning a clockwork,
clicking & clicking in between your thoughts, I'm
talking about the handywork of clocks,
the clanging and banging
and clacking of thoughts, hours and hours between each tick,
slinking and sinking between each tock, I'm talking about
how endless, how endless
this clock.

The vegetarian

Already I remember the good and the bad. Your smile
at all the right things. The smell of appam flying
towards us. The waiter setting it down between us. *Clang.* You ask

for a bottle of coke. I ask for two glasses of water and one more
spoon. Behind us, tables of families are digging with their whole hands
smeared orange. I am the only woman
wearing pants. *You'll have the chicken,*

right? You'll love it. I'm thinking of the vegetable stew because it is
coconutty. I'm thinking if I remember I'm vegetarian, and I do remember
you have no money. *Sure, I'll share the curry.* You're wearing your black

sweater, hair spread in clumps against your forehead. I take my fingers
and sweep them back. You're looking
at the menu you love so much. I am
bursting with scenes I need to put on the table, *listen, remember Rahul?*

Yesterday he had a whole pizza. Listen, I think I want to leave this job,
it's become so boring; my brain is falling. Listen,
Chait is coming home tomorrow.
I'm so happy, maybe I'll bring him here,

he likes chicken. Listen, I feel exhausted. But I don't say anything
because it's your turn. Because you have shushed my words. *Shhh,*
everyone is staring at us. Because you have erased my fingers

reaching for yours. Because what I want to share
is not chicken. So I pull back into my mouth,
ball into one large ball, and swallow.

Five stages

Is it odd to extend responsibility
for my body? To say these eyes
were ok before you came
and when you turned me on
the water broke. To say my body isn't really
mine, it is an amalgamation
of all the bodies that have ever touched,
entered, stroked. Is it odd
to say my lip is curling, snot is forming globules
and my head is stiff
from you entering in and out of it?
(I hadn't known it was possible. And if I had,
would I have allowed it?) Consider how malleable
to be so affected. You called me sensitive.
But I think this smashing of bones,
this routinic tumbling down five stages
of grief, then cycling back
to stage one, is manic, and my doctor
hasn't found me a name for it.
The problem
is I don't know the practice of stopping
when breath becomes so sharp
you can hear it chipping at your alveoli
as it filters in. This breath
that has no you in it. When we would lie
next to each other, our mouths
facing into, then it was in the air I suppose, the warning,
the heating up of noses, that this wasn't really
my body, that I was prone to surrendering.

Whole moons

When you take a piece
                of the whole
it is still
        whole.

The piece still whole
        and the whole
                still whole.

And if you give this whole
to someone

it is still whole.

    The very first whole
is still whole.
            God

is the first whole.
            And maybe love
is part of it

and maybe so are your knees,

your crooked, swollen-
under-the-bone knees

and maybe whole
        is who I feel

when the backs of your knees
flatten, then leave
                two shiny pools
        running
on my skin.

Musculature

You have left again.
Taking care of myself is all that I am left with.
You always leave. I use expletives
like always and never and I know
they don't make sense and they irritate you so much. I am here
paralyzed by fixing you into an asshole
and loving you simultaneously. And I know
the heart is a muscle, but how many times is it breaking?
Ask me what I am, and I will tell you I am some sort of
surrender. Some sort of fist opening into palm
and thrusting. Is this the muscular version
of breaking? This stretching outward into the shape
of your body and then when you leave,
this giant hollow-shaped you that is
left. Like slept-in jeans and the body inside
evaporated. I want to take care of myself. Only. Remember this,
muscles are sinuous and tenuous
and can take the shape of my body. I lit the eight
tealights in our balcony, rosewood and cedarwood,
did you never love me? I looked out at them and the smoggy
cold scent of cracker fumed into my nose and you were there
in the mist, mooning tall and large. But I had to hold
around my chest, breathing smaller and smaller
into my arms.

Because it is hot

we chug our beer in the auto
on our way to your one room
apartment. You lift my body back,
press me into the door. My tongue
is sour, sweat lines my neck,
drips into my breast.
You exhale, char
off my jeans, singe
my kurta off, you want this.
Your fingers twang
my panty, teeth
grow out of my neck.
You want to rub my clit. Higher,
higher, I whisper, but it's too high,
not low enough, no, you want this.
My neck twists into a C,
head fixes on the door. Behind
your shoulder, I watch
your empty bed, watch
my body walk across, watch
my body seep into the mattress. In front
of your shoulder, I stand
hooked to the door. Your palms
grip my shoulder, flip
me over, you want this, bend
me forward, *thump*
                    thump
                            thump my forehead
hits the door.

**Love the feeling is nothing without
Love the doing-word**

Because I had never seen palm trees
growing wild in the north,
because they spurted so tall

in your grandmother's city,
I thought we too could grow
in unlikely places.

You said the scars will fade
but on my knee there is a star
brown from twenty years ago and it shows

no signs of leaving. Is it funny
that I saw nothing of the city
except the Heart Hospital? It's blinking red

opposite my hotel window.
That they assigned me twin beds,
each with its own duvet.

That I'll never again say
my boyfriend is Bihari. That a few steps from here
is your grandfather's library

where I thought you will take me some day.
Yes, I imagined it. Floor to ceiling
black wood shelves lined with red spines,

dust under our feet, your fingers finding
book after book after book. Because I asked you
to stop hurting me when I didn't know how

to stop hurting myself. Because I hated it
when anyone sat across from me at dinner
and said, he is not a good guy. I could not

agree. Not even when I punched
your cheek.

Apparitions

Outside the door that changes nameplates
just before my appointment—the last one
for the day at 5:36 p.m.—it now says Plastic Surgeon.

Before this, I didn't know that love
could ferry my bones to hospitals.
Across the door is the Minor Operating Theatre

where other bones are ferried but on real stretchers,
wounds cradled in browning blankets. I am still
calling it love even after I told you, 'I know

what love feels like. My brother loves me.
My mother loves me.' and I am still watching you
drag this stretcher, now long after

you have left. Just like I would see Dadaji after he died,
leaning on his side of the bed, forward and backward
with prayer beads in hand. After I howled

through four nights, Dadi lay me down and covered me
in Dadaji's blanket. '*Ab se akele mat sona.*' I think
that's when she too stopped seeing him.

The girl with a rod

You are sitting in our school bus
on the bench with the other boys.
I am wearing my cage
under the blue uniform.
Plastic girdle holding
pelvis and stomach.
Your sweater is off,
mine is still on.
I have wrapped a blue scarf
on the iron around my neck.
I am smelling of sweat. Chin itchy
from resting on it. You are watching
my neck face forward. You ask
if I have a rod
in my back. The other boys laugh.
Main bas pooch raha hoon,
bura mat maan na, you say.
You are holding my eyes. I am
not ready for this.
I cross my arms on a rod.
Nahin,
there is nothing
inside my back.
I lean on the seat
and the iron
goes *creak*,
then crack.

What your doctor will not tell you:

On the days your intercostal muscles are tired from holding up,
choose a semi-soft pillow and throw them.
Hard-back chairs will hurt no matter what.
Arches will come easily to you—a curved spine knows how to bend.
You will develop an affinity to mountains.
Rest will mean those nights when your left rib and right rib
are touching the bed in one line.
Do not listen to 'Sexy Back'.
Road trips will mean calcification.
There is no right bra size.
There will be men (and women) who will trail your vertebrae.
You will accumulate an assortment of pillows.
Bones are not love-handles.
On Sunday afternoons, you will want a right-rib-hump massage—
find someone with large palms.
Do not listen to 'Sexy Back'.

What your doctor will tell you:

Forty-five degrees to the right. Thoraco-lumbar.
Cut open. Iron rod. Stitch. Small
Surgery. Milwaukee. *Kuch nahin hota hai.* Insert. Spine
Still growing. MRI. Pregnancy. Girls grow till seventeen.
Iron. Curved. Rod. *Sharma ji hain, vo* fitting *kar denge.*
No known cause. Stop tennis classes.
In eight years when she's twenty. Brace. No
Known cause. Twenty-two hours. *Lacheeli.*
Push ribs in place. *Phir vo* slouch *nahin karegi.*
L6-L7. Bent-back X-ray. Idiopathic. S shape. Take off your shirt.
Are you wearing a baniyaan? All normal activities. Surgery.
Bohot ladkiyan aati hain. Aap se bhi chhoti-chhoti.

Plunge

The year I decided
I no longer wanted men,

my body also decided
that it did. I could not rub poems

against my clit. The words melted
like dead ant heads. Their toes

curling to the floor. My belly
grew softer and the button

hung convex. I plucked wild
Syngonium from the park's sidewalk.

Digging the hardened mud
with a *karchchi*. Trying to locate the roots

whole. In return, the knobbly
mouths threw up sand

that clung like diamonds
to my clavicle bone, shimmering

with sweat. When I plunged them
through the mouth of a beer

bottle, the roots
contracted into each other

to slide through its neck
before bursting forth—boom

into the vastness
of its belly. For a second, I thought they

believed
they were going to open

into air.

Up

I am standing behind a white curtain,
pressing the rewind button,
humming to 'Up' by Shania Twain. I hide

because this is my father's cassette
and I am only ten. Shania's body meets somebody's
tongue. She asks me to go Up.

I sing along to Shania, (*it only hurts*
when I'm breathing) slow-dance
with my arms behind the curtain, (*my heart*

only breaks when it's beating)
I am ten, but I am full,
overflowing with the limbs of loving.

Big

I am ten. I stand
under the shade of the tallest tree
at the centre of our garden.

My brother does cartwheels.
I try to, but
I am big.

I rolly-polly down the hill—
fold my knees into fetus position,
loosen my neck and push

my weight forward. I tumble
sky grass sky grass sky grass
thump, tree trunk.

Between every roll
I pull down layers
of shirt and sweater

sky grass pull sky grass pull
I cannot bear my flesh.
Who taught me this?

Enter a garden in new delhi

at 1 p.m.
all around you there are
men

spread
men spread out
spread all around

legsflopping backssprawling
handsscratching bodiesrelaxing

men spread
in circles and triangles
rose beds and grass rectangles

enter your body
here in this garden
of men
spread

Sometimes we are not people

we are acid rain, corroding whoever stands under our frame.
Umbrellas are no use when we blow against the wind.
Sometimes we are not people,
we enchantress, we murderess, we death. We curse at Brahma.
At whoever crosses the Lakshman Rekha.
We hold our hair above their thigh and smack. Sometimes
we are not kind, we are seething like a falling star hot
with gravity. We burn holes in mountains.
Sometimes we are not
Mother Teresa, we are Kali drunk on champagne,
tearing our lungs and your ear drums. Most of the time
we are not forgiving,
(we take up swords sharp as our needles)
most of the time we have no reason.

'You need a strong man'

I need a soft man like ice cream chocolate brown melting
in my mouth a soft man who knows to breathe into my
ears and tug at the lobes a soft man curled into a comma
against my back a soft man wiping water down his eye a
soft man flopping on the divan after a long meeting at work
a soft man breaking into words like lovely like I love you
like I need you a soft man belly pressing under palm warm
belly warm curls of black hair soft man folding shawarma
halfway then bottomway a soft man with fingers wrapping
into mine like softly falling cotton.

I will constantly choose my blood

I will grip down my mattress, go
into labour with myself. I will
give birth to men, give birth
to women. I will leak fast, leak slow,
leak to the beat of my umbo. I will eject
a river down my thigh. I will
splatter maroon on the walls. I will live
before he enters and after
he pulls out. I will shed
in a mortar-pestle and grind,
plug the paste on my *maang*. I will
constantly choose my blood.

Silent night

B and I at the Chocolateria,
dunking our anxieties, churro-shaped,
into a pot of hot chocolate. Outside,

the fog settling in wet droplets
on the backs of cars. Inside, Christmas Carols
playing on a loop. B and I know all the words

from school. Mrs Kumar, first name Frances,
would squat on the floor with a xylophone.
We would take our mango seeds, dried

into tiny drums, and tap-tap-tap-tap,
beat them with pencils.
She would sit behind her piano

in a neat stool. Her arms plugging
the music, rising with *Sii-iii-*
lent night, then softening

into *Shhhhephards quake,*
at the sight. Since then,
I never really came

through a door, singing,
and laughing. Laughing and singing.
Instead, my father had me flatten

onto a study table. 'Laugh softly'
he would say, softly,
like a cotton flower,

plucked by a wind, softly,
like a fresh bud, unopen. 'No petals',
he would say. Stop showing me

your petals. All that red,
all that expanse. How dare you
open and take

those lung-fulls of air?
B had a father too.
He had a thick mustache

and those shearing scissors
he used to snip
all the mouths of buds. B and I learnt

that silence lived
outside of Christmas
nights. We perfected the words,

*holy infant so tender
and mild.* We rubbed mango seeds
between our palms,

knew the absence
of drumming, knew even that.

We keep going to SDA because it is half way

(For B)

Occasionally you say, *come home, it's been too long.*
Occasionally I say, *let's do a sleepover.*

You show me the only way to line eyes with kajal.

I never wash it off before sleeping,
you close your eyelids around the black tip
and swipe your finger *rightleftrightleft.*

I spend five minutes lining my top lid.
Then I sleep. While you and the other girls chat.
I sleep like a dead body. You are terrified.
You pull the white sheet off my chin, laughing.

I do not sleep like that next to men.

Learning to leave men

This is my dream and I will leave
any man who cannot hold it. It started
with father. I left one morning,

folding my books into cardboard cartons.
The men he called to lift, brought a truck larger
than I had space to fill. He walked

barefoot among the closing
of my room, his face pink and my body
a serpent. I shed some of his skin

and left it among my old
Syngonium. I never came back
to take them. In the new balcony, I found hoopoes

and six trees, guarding my entry
into a new world. B helped unpack
the books. We dusted each one,

lining the shelf with paper, mixing pink,
fluorescent orange, and green, lodged
each book, straight-spined, poetry with poetry,

fiction all random. I left my childhood
books behind, their stories still webbing
my father's walls.

Perennial

It's the white paper notices stuck in the handle of our main-door
(another two old people are gone), that remind me they had mornings

sitting on green iron benches, fingers to their noses,
pressing the right hole first and breathing from the left,

then the other way round, they filtered air.
It's always a group of Dadajis, ha-ha-ha-ha, palms thrown skyward,

or Dadis who bring yoga mats, blue purple green
and lay them on the grass: one behind the other beside the other.

They stretch in kurta-pajama and sneakers. It's 6 a.m.
and I've just tumbled out of bed. The yoga instructor is a young man,

with his hair slicked-back. He walks barefoot between the mats.
I think even the trees in this park are old. They have barks

the thickness of ten Dadis hugging each other.
From my balcony I see them moving. Some are brisk-

walking like cars circling a round-about. I like to think they are happy
in this small park holding their bodies. They ask me,

remember leaves and petals? Open their palms. Every
house has clippings
of money plant and succulents: aloe vera pots with octopus
tendrils. Here I am

the slow upward glide of necks
in the morning, into it I shed like the thaw of belonging.

First thunderstorm

My heart is thudding as I pull out of the taxi,
tap the stairs, laughing

at the suddenness, the thrill
of being locked, outside, hitting
key to the door, jingling as my hair blows

cold and wet. My toes are drenched. I enter.
Sit in a corner scooping smaller and smaller

portions of blueberry cheesecake. The ficus
is knocked off the ledge. The succulents are weeping.
Outside and my heart is thudding

for them. I pull behind the walls,
huddle into corners, drag the orange pots.
Cold and wet. My heart is thudding somebody

to press against. I let the ants in. The little moths
with speckled wings. They too are curling like this.

ACKNOWLEDGEMENTS

I am very grateful to Arundhathi Subramaniam and the jury for selecting my manuscript as the beneficiary of the Khiwani Bequest.

I acknowledge the following literary magazines for publishing previous versions of poems from this manuscript—*The Bangalore Review, The Bombay Literary Magazine, The Punch Magazine,* and *Bengaluru Review.*

This book wouldn't have been possible without the relentless love and encouragement of the following people—Mom, Papa, Chaitanya, Mausi, Nani, Dadi, Nana, Dada, Bishnupriya, Neymat, Kandala, Sudha, Aditi, my main writing group (Kamal, Neha, Shalini, Vasudha, Abhay), Urvashi, Chandrahas, Tara, my Goa Bound writers' group, Anmol, Safeya, Prabhat, Simi, Shikha, Manmeet, Manika and Vishruta. I couldn't have done any of it without you.

I am grateful for the brilliant team at Speaking Tiger for making this book come together.

www.ingramcontent.com/pod-product-compliance
Lightning Source LLC
LaVergne TN
LVHW040518200726
843493LV00017B/2442